A Long Walk to the Throne

HRH King Okogyeman Kobina Amissah I

Greatness University

Greatness University Publishers
London, UK
www.greatnessuniversity.co.uk
ISBN: 978-1-913164-15-7
ISBN-13: 978-1-913164-15-7

HRH KING OKOGYEMAN KOBINA AMISSAH 1

Dedication

To dad and mum,

you always taught me to dream.

To the I Change Nations global family,

thank you for giving me the opportunity to serve you.

Contents

Acknowledgements

HRH King Okogyeman Kobina Amissah I
Founder of iChange Nations & Godfather of the World Civility Movement

HRH King Okogyeman Kobina Amissah I

I would like to start by remembering the people I have met in my journey. I remember going to Lusaka, Zambia to honour President Kenneth Kaunda. Whilst seated in his lounge and at 94 years old, he ran down the stairs with his white handkerchief coming to meet us. During our encounter, I asked him, "What is the key to the world?" He replied, "Young man, it is peace. And peace is priceless... You are a great man."

When you hear these words coming from this great man, it is humbling. There is a general rule which is: no person becomes great by himself or herself. Nobody wins alone. So, at the start of this acknowledgements, I would like to express my sincere thanks to the people who have taken this long walk to the throne with me. Special thanks to my wife Mrs Mary Alice Rivers for her tireless sacrifice of being without whenever I am on my national and international engagements. My wife has supported me 100 percent in what I am doing. All I can say is nothing is possible without my wife.

Dr Robin Lococo has been an administrator for me over 25 years. She has been through the good, the bad, the ugly, and the indifference. She has never turned away. She has always been on course. When you first start out, it with sticks and stones. With sticks and stones, we built I Change Nations Global house.

When I Change Nations took an educational twist, Dr Michal Pitzl came in as Chancellor and put her money where her mouth was. She has built a phenomenal institution and without her, the United Graduate College and Seminary International would not be existing today.

Then, Dr Donni Pitzl carried the ball when everything turned a different way and carried us along the way.

My sister Stephanie Anne Rivers. She was a pillar in my whole life. Then, my dad and mother. They always taught me to dream. They always stood behind in whatever I did. I am grateful for their lives and the legacy to dream they left in me.

Then, the international I Change Nations Family. I am grateful for having worked with the best people in the world. They are all priceless to me. I would like to give distinguish recognition to President Pierre Nkurunziza, his wife Denise Nkurunziza, and the rest of his family. Special thanks to Dr Albert Nasasagare who taught me how to be diplomatic.

I am forever indebted to these and all the people I have met on my long walk to the throne for the contributions they have made in my life.

Introduction

Professor Patrick Businge
Founder of Greatness University

Thank you, Greatness University, for giving me the opportunity to introduce this book on the journey that HRH King Okogyeman Kobina Amissah I (also known as Sir Clyde Rivers) has taken to his throne in Kuotukwa Kingdom in Ghana. As you turn over the pages of this legacy book, you will discover his royal greatness that is rooted in his divine calling and his civility humanitarianism that continue to kindle the hearts and minds of those who encounter him. It is my hope that as you read this book, you will not just go through the chapters but grow. In doing so, you will learn from his life so that you become a human being who manifests civility and royalty.

In the first Chapter of this book, you will learn about Africa: the ancestral home of Sir Okogyeman Kobina Amissah I. You will also discover the long walk to slavery that the ancestors of Sir Clyde Rivers took from the interior of Africa through the stormy waters of the Atlantic Ocean to the plantations in America. Reflecting on the experiences of slavery, you will discover how HRH Sir Clyde Rivers discovered his greatness and what he meant in saying: "In this long walk to the throne, it is vital understand that one of my ancestors came to America in a boat and I fly back to Africa in a plane in a seat. This is a major paradigm shift and adjustment. In this long walk to the throne, I did not experience what my ancestors experienced."

After this historical background, Chapter 2 offers a reflection on Sir Clyde River's divine mission. We will reflect on how Sir Clyde Rivers' coming from America to Africa was not controlled by human beings but a mission ordained by God. He has made a joyful journey to Africa as a humble servant and steward of God.

The third chapter maps out what the 30 year long walk that Sir Clyde Rivers has made to the throne has entailed. You will discover the various walks he has taken as a Dean at UGCSI, Ambassador at Large for Burundi, Global Chairman for OPAD, Golden Rule Ambassador, Godfather of World Civility, and Founder of I Change Nations.

The final Chapter of this book titled *You Walked with Me* recognizes some of the people who have walked with Sir Clyde Rivers. Without going through a very long list, three people are used as examples to illustrate his message. These include H.E. President Pierre Nkurunziza, Dr Myles Monroe, and Professor Albert Nasasagare.

This book ends with a brief reflection on the legacy of greatness that Sir Clyde Rivers has created. Greatness University theorises legacy as not what we leave with people when we are gone but what we live in them. As you read this book, you will discover that Sir Clyde River's legacy lies in his selfless service. He is a **Selfless Servant Leader** who is not in love with power but in love with humanity. His legacy as a leader does not lie in his desire to lead others with authority but in his ability to serve others in a selfless way.

The famous Theologian St. Augustine wrote, 'If you should ask me what the ways of God are, I would tell you that the first is humility, the second is humility, and the third is humility. Not that there are no other precepts to give, but if humility does not precede all that we do, our efforts are fruitless.' As you read this book on the long walk to the throne, you will experience Sir Clyde Rivers as a man of great humility. Humility is one of his ways to serve as a Dean at the UGCSI, as Ambassador at Large for Burundi, as a Global Chairman of OPAD, as Golden Rule Ambassador, as Godfather of world Civility, as Founder of I Change Nations, and now as a King of Development in Ghana. Sir Clyde Rivers does not only teach with his words but also with his life. This is what makes him one of the World's Greatest **Civility Humanitarian**.

Following in the footsteps of the great son of Africa Nelson Mandela who said, 'Education is the most powerful weapon that you can use to change the world;' Sir Clyde Rivers has used education in form of training and mentoring to create a legacy of service, civility, and royalty. This legacy is being passed on to individuals, families, nations, and kingdoms. This is why he has been recognised by Greatness University London in creating the Sir Clyde Rivers Presidential Greatness and Civility Humanitarian Award. Read this book and be transformed by the life and legacy of Sir Clyde Rivers.

A Painful Journey to America

Africa's Greatness

It can be asserted that HRH King Okogyeman Kobina Amissah I's walk to the throne started in Africa even before his birth. This is because his walk is intrinsically link to Africa on various levels.

On a scientific level, Africa, which is currently the home of approximately 1.5 billion people, is the birthplace of humanity. Scientists are certain that homo sapiens first evolved in Africa. They tell us that every human being can trace their genetic ancestry to Africa. The latest scientific research points to the fact that all human beings are likely to have African ancestors. On a very simplistic level, all human beings are Africans by origin.

On a royalty level, Africa is the amphitheatre of royal civilization. In Africa we find ancient kingdoms such as Kemet that had its civilization in the Nile Valley over 5000 years ago. Also referred to as Ancient Egypt or Egypt of the Pharaohs, Kemet is best known for its great monuments, beautiful architecture, complex engineering, and the timeless pyramids. The Egyptians also produced early types of paper, devised a written script, and developed a calendar. They made important contributions in various branches of mathematics such as geometry and algebra. They equally made important contributions to mechanics, philosophy, and agriculture. In medicine, the Egyptians understood the body's dependence on the brain more than 1,000 years before the Greeks. Today, Ancient Egypt is not only associated with scientific developments, engineering, mathematics, architecture, medicine but also with early political developments such as state formation and monarchy.

On a historic level, Africa was the first centre of human civilization. Even before the rise of Kemet, an earlier kingdom of Ta Seti existed in Nubia: the present-day

Sudan. Some of the world's great civilisations flourished in Africa such as Kush in the present-day Sudan, Axum in the present-day Ethiopia, and others in Mali, Zimbabwe, and the rest of Africa.

An article titled *Africa before Transatlantic Enslavement* reveals that the African continent continued its own path of development without significant external intervention until the 15th century. Before this period, Africans participated in extensive international trade networks and in trans-oceanic travel with India, China, and other parts of Asia. It adds that:

> A North African conquest of the Iberian peninsular began in the 8th century and led to the occupation of much of Spain and Portugal for several centuries. This Muslim invasion re-introduced much of the knowledge of the ancient world to Europe and linked it much more closely with North and West Africa. It was gold from the great empires of West Africa, such as Ghana, Mali and Songhay, which provided the means for the economic take off of Europe in the 13th and 14th centuries and aroused the interest of Europeans in western Africa. Indeed, it was the wealth of West Africa, especially as a source of gold, that encouraged the voyages of the early European explorers. By the 15th century the existence of great kingdoms and empires in Africa were exceptional rather than typical.

Most importantly African societies followed their own patterns of development before the onset of transatlantic slave trade. This history of greatness acts as a tapestry on which Sir Clyde Rivers begins his long walk to the throne.

A Long Walk to Slavery

Historically, the transatlantic slave trade in the 15th century saw many people from Africa taken into slavery to various continents especially America and Europe. This trade disrupted Africa's culture, civilisation, and development. It also led to the loss of lives, depopulation of the African continent, and the departure of people who could have contributed to Africa's development. Though slavery was prevalent in African societies before the arrival of Europeans, the arrival of Europeans increased the demand of slaves. This led to people being kidnapped, sold off and shipped to various destinations.

The Encyclopaedia Britannica notes that European buyers who mainly stayed on the African coasts waited for slaves to be brought from the interior on foot by African sellers. This journey from the interior to the coast was up to 485 km. That the captives were chained together by the ankle. Then, columns of captives were tied together by ropes around the neck and approx. 15 per cent of captives died on the long walk from the interior of Africa to its coast, and from the coast to America. The distant relatives of Sir Clyde Rivers were amongst the slaves taken to America. His relatives made a long walk to slavery to America: a foreign land where they were poorly treated.

In his book titled *The Sorrows of Slavery*, the historic black poet Benjamin Franklin Burum has a collection of poems that gives us a glimpse into what happened during the journey to America and their experience of slavery once they arrived on the American soil. In his drawing and poem titled *Decreasing Cargo*, he describes how slaves were perceived as unneeded cargo and they were sometimes drowned on their way to America.

Photo Credits: Benjamin F Burum, The Sorrows of Slavery

Here is the poem from Benjamin's book *The Sorrows of Slavery*:

> *Today they brought 50 of us above deck,*
>
> *And just when my eyes began to focus, as I began to look around,*
>
> *A slippery substance is placed beneath our feet causing all 50 of us to fall-down.*
>
> *"Decrease the cargo by 50!" is what someone had said,*
>
> *As we slide into the water, chained together, I knew that all 50 of us would be dead,*
>
> *Resting on the ocean floor, as we all fight and struggle,*
>
> *Knowing that we will be free in a different way, with the decrease in oxygen bubbles,*
>
> *Is this right? The thing I need to know!*
>
> *When 50 slaves lose their lives, the Whiteman calls it* DECREASING CARGO. *(p4).*

Reflecting on the sorrows of slavery, the concept of all human beings having equal worth, the belief that all human beings are created in the image and likeness of God, the ethic that all human beings are to be loved treated with respect were completely alien. In other words, civility was not the order of the day. For instance, like the slave masters, some of the kings in Africa believed that slavery was from God. In the BBC article titled **'My Nigerian great-grandfather sold slaves' - BBC News** states that when King Bonny heard that slave trade was being abolished by the British in the late 19th Century and early 20th Century, he said "That is the verdict of our oracle and our priests. They say that your country, however great, can never stop a trade ordained by God."

In interview with Professor Patrick Businge, Sir Clyde Rivers noted, "My relatives come from Africa. One of the things I now know is that someone in my family lineage came from Africa to America as a slave. They came and served as a slave. This is a critical component in my long walk." He goes on to say that "I grew up in America with no working knowledge of Africa except the pictures I saw on the TV. The information that came to me about Africa I just received. As I was making my first trip to Kampala Uganda, I thought I was going to find monkeys on the tarmac. That's the image I had seen about Africa. When I got there, I realized it is not this way at all." It is in the midst of the realization of this painful walk to slavery that his ancestors took that Sir Clyde Rivers discovered his greatness.

Finding my Greatness

In the first section of this chapter, we discovered Africa as the birthplace of humanity. We noticed it as the centre of ancient civilization. We also visualized Africa as the amphitheatre of royalty. We also got a glimpse of the long walk to slavery that the ancestors of Sir Clyde Rivers might have taken from the interior of Africa to the Atlantic Ocean coast where they were sold and sent off to America. Reading the poem written by Benjamin Burum, we got a snapshot of the sorrow and suffering slaves might have experienced on their way from the coast of Africa to the interior of America. We also conceptualized Africa as the ancestral home of Sir Clyde Rivers.

As we reflect on the greatness of Sir Clyde Rivers in this section, it is critical that we notice the parallels between him and his ancestors from Africa. In the first instance, the coming of his ancestors to America was initiated by human beings. His return to Africa was initiated by God. His ancestors came to America as working slaves. HRH goes back to Africa as a king of development. His ancestors came to America as servants to human beings. He goes back to Africa as a servant to God. His ancestors made the long walk to slavery in the plantations. HRH takes the long walk to service on the royal throne. His ancestors were dishonoured in their servitude. HRH was honoured in his service. His ancestors lost their freedom to human beings. HRH lost his freedom to God. This is where his greatness lies: in his obedience to the vision of civility for all that God showed him.

The Roots of Civility

Sir Clyde Rivers grew up in a loving family with his father, mother, and siblings. As his father was in the military, he remembers his early years characterized by travelling around the USA with his siblings and moving from one military base to another where his father worked. Thinking about these years, Sir Clyde Rivers narrates:

> In the military bases, everybody lived together. I grew up in a multi-cultural community. I had black friends. I had white friends. I had Hispanic friends. I had Indian friends. I grew in a very balanced society.

This demonstrates that from early on in his life, Sir Clyde Rivers was exposed to people from different races. As had friends from other racial groups, he knew the value of the racial and ethnic diversity created by the cosmopolitan places he grew up in. These racial differences did not constrain him but created an environment where he was a friend to all.

Sir Clyde Rivers also respected people for who they were. This led him to treat people with respect. As we shall explore further in the next chapter, this was the foundation for his work in civility. He says,

> I was a good athlete, but I had an awkward group of friends. I was friend to everyone… So, in my home, we were taught that people are people. We were taught to treat people with respect. Because this was part of my life, I treat all people with civility. I remember having a meeting with Janet Museveni. She said, "Dr Rivers I want to thank you because you treat everyone the same. You treated the leader of this country and the poor in the same way."

This is a clear testament that as a young person, Sir Clyde Rivers was civil to all. Today, he continues to live this message of civility using his life and actions. This is the message he takes around the world: be civil to all. This is the solution that he has for the world: civility for all.

We have come the end of this first part of this book where we have explored how Sir Clyde Rivers' ancestors in Africa were sold into slavery and took the look journey to America. In the next chapter, we delve into his mission of civility that led HRH Sir Clyde Rivers to be given the title 'Godfather of World Civility.' Let us join him as he elicits the key signposts that have allowed him to take on the royal mission to Africa.

A Royal Mission to Africa

HRH at the Door of Return (previously the Door of No Return) at Cape Coast Castle, Ghana

Discovering his Gift

'I was special needs but I was also an elite basketballer.'

Sir Clyde Rivers

Apart from civility, Sir Clyde Rivers had other gifts that helped him live his greatness. During his schooling, Sir Clyde Rivers was identified as having special education needs. He grew up whilst being labelled as a special child. This led him to be educated differently and separately from other children in the schools that were considered normal. Having special needs did not have a good connotation at that time. For instance, children with special needs were considered subnormal, imbecile, mentally retarded, mad, stupid, outcast, etc. During the interview, HRH Sir Clyde Rivers remarked:

> I used to write upside down. That had put me in a special education classroom. In elementary school, all other children would go to another school, and I was bused into another school. I studied with children who had special needs. We were considered outcast because of our differences. However, I was always an anomaly among the outcast. Everyone was cheering me up on Tuesdays and Fridays at the basketball match. Then, they were laughing at me on Mondays, Wednesdays and Thursdays as I sneaked into the special needs' door to go for my lessons. It was called the outcast door. I belonged to the outcast group who got outcast education.

This testimony reveals that Sir Clyde Rivers was excluded from the normal classroom as he was perceived as not having the academic ability. He was however included in the basketball team as he was perceived normal on the sports pitch. In other words, he was considered both a negative statistic in the classroom and a positive statistic in sports.

Sir Clyde Rivers remembers that in his first basketball match at college, his team beat Oregon State. As years passed by, his success in basketball increased and so was his fame. As a good basketballer, he was elevated to a different stage. He received division 1 basketball scholarship. Each time he went to play basketball, he was looked at as number one. In some of the matches, Sir Clyde Rivers was watched by over 18,000 people. Using his talent and gift placed him in the celebrity class. This implies that when you use talent, no human being can put you in the outcast class. Your gifts are vehicles that will take you many to places. Your gifts are keys which will open many doors. As seen from the photograph on the next page taken in 1986, HRH went on to co-host sports radio with the then Miss America Charlene Wells during the Utah- BYU football game.

This kind of treatment highlights the normality and abnormality dichotomy and how it relates to inclusion and exclusion in society. In this case, Sir Clyde Rivers was excluded by human beings who saw him as not normal. Just like abnormality, normality is a construct. Normality requires abnormality as they are binary opposites. There are various models of normality and abnormality. For instance, the statistical model is based on standard deviation. In this model, normality is defined in terms of the 'normal zone' which accounts for 68 percent of all data in the normal distribution curve and abnormality is associated with low statistical frequency (Wilkinson & Roberts, 2006). This leads to the conception of normality as normal and abnormality as abnormal. Using this model, those who are normal are included and those who are abnormal are excluded.

However, with God, there is no separation between normal and abnormal. God's image is in everyone irrespective of their ability or disability. In the case of Sir Clyde Rivers, he was included by God. Though he was marginalized in education and considered an outcast in the eyes of human beings, he was unique in the eyes of God. He was gifted by God and, with the help of his parents, he discovered his unique gifts. These gifts acted as vehicles to embark on the long walk to the throne.

Sir Clyde Rivers is aware of this uniqueness and giftedness as he passionately commented during the interview:

> In my youth I had two special components: special needs and elite basket baller. My high school in Victorville, California: that is 40 years on, my basketball legacy is still there. I am still the leading scorer in basketball. The history hasn't changed that much since I was there. My gifting was different from my academic endeavour. God's gift has outshined definitions put in me at a young age. There is greatness in every child and their greatness might not come through the academic route.

This means that as a young man, Sir Clyde Rivers knew he was a special you. He discovered his gift. He developed his gift. He led with his gift. Looking back on the story of Sir Clyde Rivers and connecting the dots, our gifts show up at a young age. As a parent, how are you helping your child discover their area of gifting so that they take their own walk to their throne? As seen in Sir Clyde Rivers life, his gifting in basketball has outshined the definitions put on him at a very young age. He has greatness in him but his struggles are overshadowing this greatness. He says, "My parents told me I was number one, and I believed it." What helped him was that his parents saw the greatness in him. There is greatness in every child and their academic success might not capture this greatness.

When his Sir Clyde Rivers was asked about what motivated him, he said:

> I am not supposed to be where I am today. Basketball became a passion

> of my life. It made it possible for me to be where I am today… I was in special needs classes in junior, elementary, and high school. The passion for basketball allowed me to get good grades… I managed to get my university degree from the University of Utah. So, I call this the power of passion. I was passionate on basketball, and nothing was going to stop me.

This testament demonstrates that no great work can be done without passion. Passion allows us to overcome our limitations and do our best. So, looking at the early life of Sir Rivers and comparing it with that he has achieved today, it is incomprehensible. His life is an example of a passionate human being. His life unifies the perceived human limitations with the greatness in each one of us. It is passion that has pushed Sir Clyde Rivers to leave the comfort of his home in America to embark on a royal mission to Africa.

The Calling to Africa

After discovering his gift and living it with passion in the United States of America, Sir Clyde Rivers heard the calling to go Africa. In the interview with Professor Patrick Businge, Sir Clyde Rivers revealed that he started to feel a special calling from the age of 17 years old. He went on to say:

> When at I was at Utah University, spirituality was part of my life. I had a green Gideon Bible which I would read a sentence or chapter no matter what time of the day. Then, whilst doing my sophomore year, Andy Parker - a football player at Utah and a born-again Christian - started talking to me about God. He sowed seeds in my life that led me to Jesus Christ. Form my traditional Catholic faith, I became a born-again Christian. When I got born again, I was converted. When I got converted, God became my whole life. I knew right from wrong. I now had two passions in life: basketball and Jesus. The minute basketball ended; Jesus started. I lived my whole life for Jesus. From this point onwards, I knew that I was going to serve God and Jesus for the rest of my life.

Sir Clyde Rivers did not start straight away serving God in ministry. After Utah University, he worked at Goodyear Tyres for approx. 6 years. He narrates that whilst driving home one evening from work, he heard the voice of God telling him to stop working in the tyre industry and start ministry. Heeding to the divine calling, he quit his job the next month. Remembering the moment, Sir Clyde Rivers narrated:

> On the same day when I resigned from my job and come home, my dad asked me to go to church with him. I accepted and went to church with

> him. My dad was not a very spiritual man when I was growing up. However, when he got saved, his entire life was committed to the Lord. Reaching there, Pastor James Markham was speaking. In my head I said, "This is what I want to do with my life."

In 1994, he started Miracle Faith Church in Victorville, California. This was a non-denominational ministry that brought people back to God. Despite having spent 15 years ministering at this church, it was not growing. It remained small with a handful of Christians.

Few years later, a prophecy from a man of God was to change his perspective of ministry and destination of his calling. In 1999, he was in a church where Prophet Kim Clement happened to be. Whilst in a church service, Prophet Kim Clement prophesied over his life. He called him out and stretching his hands over him, Prophet Kim Clement said:

> You Mr Afro-American, there is more Africa in you than America. God says, "I am going to send you to Africa. You are going to dance with those people because you are a first-class warrior. When you return to Africa, God is going to give you 5 different regions. He is going to give you dominion and power. Take it and its yours."

These were the exact words of the prophecy from a south African, Kim Clement: a singer, songwriter, author and pastor in Durban. Sir Clyde Rivers says that Prophet Kim Clement was a man that could hear the voice of God so fast. In this case, he mediated the divine calling to Sir Clyde Rivers. 6 years later, this clarity started off his mission to Africa: Africa where he had never been and was not even in his mind.

Six years after Prophet Kim Clément's prophecy over his life, Sir Clyde Rivers made his first journey to Africa. His first trip in Africa was to Kampala in Uganda. As he boarded the plane to Uganda, lot of things might have been on his mind. His ancestors came from Africa by boat. He is going to Africa by plane. His ancestors came to America as slaves to human beings. He is going to Africa as a servant of God. Recalling his first day in Uganda, Sir Clyde Rivers said:

> I had been in ministry serving every Sunday and Wednesday in a small church in Victorville, California. As soon as I got into Africa, I am elevated. The first day I got there with my jetlag, I go invited to Pastor Robert Kayanja's church with thousands of people there. When I go in, a friend introduced me to Pastor Kayanja. Whilst there, Pastor Kayanja asks me to open the evening with a prayer on TBN TV Channel. Little did he know that my dream was to be a pastor preaching on TBN. I go into Africa, the first day I am there, God elevates my level. I go in and first day, I am on TBN doing prayer. That was a highlight in my life as I always wanted to be on TBN.

The journey to Africa was a turning point in Sir River's life. Prior to the journey, he was focused on growing his Miracle Faith Ministries in California, America. He wanted it to be the biggest ministry there. God kept my church and ministry very small for a reason. As it was a small church, Sir Clyde Rivers had a personal relationship with the people he was ministering. As he narrates,

> This humbled me and, in the end, I loved the people I was pastoring.

> God found a way to get that out of me that number 1 is not having a big church but impacting an individual. Big did not matter anymore. If you impact one person, you are number one for that person. God in 15 years taught me how to value the individual. God has a way of taking your dream, killing it and then backing his dream…. The actual day I became Honorary Ambassador of Burundi, God said you have been faithful for over 30 people, now am making you a ruler of over 10 million people. This was a new position created by President Pierre Nkurunziza. Then in June 2020, he passed away and went to be with the Lord. About 6 months after the death of President Pierre Nkurunziza, I got a call from his Royal Majesty Nana Okogyedom Eduah V of Ekumfi Koutukwa in Ghana saying, "I want you to be a Development King for my kingdom." There is a principle in all this, when you are faithful over little, you become ruler over much. This progression is based on stewardship. Good stewardship leads rulership.

According to Sir Clyde Rivers, this is how he interprets his divine calling This is what God's mission is all about. You might want to do things in your time, but it is not God's timing. His 15 years as a minister at Miracle Faith Ministries in California, USA and 15 years of serving Burundi as its honorary ambassador have now led him to become the Development King in Ghana, Africa. Africa is a continent where his ancestors had left as slaves. He is now coming back to Africa as a king.

We have come the end of this chapter. In the past two chapters titled *A Painful Journey to America* and *A Royal Mission to Africa*, we have seen the meeting point of two extremes in the life of Sir Clyde Rivers. On one end, we see human beings placing Sir Clyde Rivers in a special education school. On the other end, we see God elevating him into a celebrity basketballer. We have looked at how his ancestors in Africa were sold into slavery and took the painful journey to America. We have noticed how God Sir Clyde Rivers was rejected and placed in special needs classes. We have discovered how he has used his gifts in sports and how God has elevated him to a celebrity status in basketball. Importantly, we have learnt that Sir Clyde Rivers was excluded by human beings but was included by God. He was marginalized in education but was exulted in basketball. He was outcast in the eyes of human beings but was unique in the eyes of God. He was treated in uncivil ways, but he chose to treat all people with civility. Based on this, we are now ready to ponder on the journey that HRH Clyde Rivers made from America to Africa in the next chapter of this book. Let us join him as he elicits the key signposts that he has encountered in this 30-year journey.

A Long Walk to the Throne

In the First Part of this book, we discovered that the coming of Sir Clyde Rivers' ancestors to America was controlled by human being. They made a painful journey to America where they experience slavery and servitude. In the Second Part of this book, we have just noted that Sir Clyde Rivers' coming from America to Africa was not controlled by humans but a mission ordained by God. He has made a joyful journey to Africa as a humble servant of God. In this Third Part, we are going to discover what this long journey that ultimately has led Sir Clyde Rivers to the throne has entailed. Read and discover the various walks he has taken as a Dean at UGCSI, Ambassador at Large for Burundi, Global Chairman for OPAD, Golden Rule Ambassador, Godfather of World Civility, and Founder of I Change Nations.

As Dean at UGCSI

Sir Clyde Rivers is the Dean of the United Graduate College and Seminary International (UGCSI). UGCSI is pioneering a lifelong learning system to empower this generation and those of the future. It is called Authorship Education™, and features "Searchers" who discover their unique skills and philosophy in order to create new disciplines in education. Authorship Education ™ is founded on the principle that every human being was created with a contribution for this world.

United Graduate College and Seminary International (UGCSI) was founded in 1982 and is an online international education institution. It offers various non-traditional, online and Biblical ministry certificates and degrees. UGCSI promotes the Culture of Honor through Honorary Degrees in Humanities based on skills and philosophy, which we bestow upon highly esteemed individuals who have devoted their life's work to the betterment of humanity. UGCSI is accredited through the Worldwide Accreditation Commission of Christian Education Institutions (WWAC).

Remembering his first trip to Uganda, Sir Clyde Rivers said that whilst he was praying on his first night in Uganda, God told him that he needs to educate Africa. That God put him in touch with Dr Martin Wiser who founded the UGCSI. He was initially appointed as the international representative of UGCSI. His work with Professor Simeon Kayiwa later led to the creation of Kayiwa International University in Uganda which is the African partner of UGCSI. Here is a word from the current Chancellor of UGCSI Professor Michal P. Pitzl on her work encounter and work with Sir Clyde Rivers.

I first met His Royal Highness Sir Clyde Rivers in 2007, and little did I know that it would change my life forever. He came to speak at my church and shared his stories about working with Latin University of Theology and traveling to the continent of Africa. I am an educator and was interested in furthering my education. I also knew I wanted to work throughout the world, especially on the continent of Africa. As the service ended, I introduced myself to his Royal Highness and told him I wanted to further my education and travel with him to the continent of Africa. He was very kind and open and genuinely enjoyed talking to the people that evening. When I introduced myself and shared my vision, he told me to jump. Four months later, I was on my way to Uganda, Africa. I had no idea what my purpose was for going on that trip, and I just knew that I was supposed to go. As soon as I arrived, opportunities and doors began to open for me. The rest is history.

Since that February day in 2007, I have been working with his Royal Highness in worldwide education. I am the 2020 Global Educator of the Year and founder of the Searcherdemic Life Education model. I discovered and grew my passion as I walked the journey with His Royal Highness. I began as a student at Latin University of Theology, earning a bachelor's degree in Theology. During this time, his Royal highness showed students how to think outside the box and be 'unlimited.' He taught us that anything was possible. His assignments encouraged us to be creative and think of unlimited possibilities. The classes engaged our God-capacity as they forced us to create solutions to real-world issues.

After receiving my second bachelor's degree, I continued my education, earning my doctorate in biblical counselling at the United Graduate College and Seminary International. I started developing a curriculum for online ministry education. Again, HRH pushed me to think with an unlimited mind, practicing and creating teaching methods and bringing empowering biblical information to students on the other side of the world. UGCSI was another organization that his Royal Highness worked with at the time. At UGCSI, I was able to create learning modules as part of my education. I had the freedom to research and study the word of God and develop proposals, programs, curriculum to engage learners actively and bring biblical principles to life in the lives of people. His Royal Highness kept the vision fresh and moving every step of the way and opened doors to create what was *needed*, not just the status quo. The life education I have received by working with His Royal Highness gave me new perspectives and opened my mind to new ideas that could reach the world. I was already a public-school educator and had my master's degree in curriculum and instruction. I knew the techniques and skills to build a curriculum and instruction, but now I had the opportunity to build on life's practical stage.

The first evening I met his Royal highness in the months to follow, he spoke of being unlimited. His Royal highness is a person full of vision and possibility. When I met him, his word was 'unlimited.' That word describes all of the experiences and opportunities that have opened up to him as he has travelled the world. He has an unlimited capacity to care for people. He has an unlimited ability for new ideas and the heart to pursue the Holy Spirit of God in the process. Anyone who has had the opportunity to meet his Royal highness has experienced this unlimited enthusiasm and gift. He is changing the world by opening humanity's eyes to its unlimitedness.

Awards Ceremony at Kayiwa International University in Uganda

HRH King Okogyeman Kobina Amissah I

As Ambassador at Large for Burundi

When Sir Clyde Rivers went to Africa, he went as a preacher and educator. Overtime, he became the Ambassador at Large for Burundi: a country that was not his own. How did this happen? According to him, it was God's plans that came with the culture of honour that he had established through I Change Nations. Sir Clyde Rivers explains this thus:

> After I honoured President Museveni and the First Lady Janet Museveni, someone mentioned to me President Pierre Nkurunziza. I researched about him and found that he is a believer who had turned his country around using Christian principles such as reconciliation. President was such a down to earth and touchable person. I learnt one thing from him: **Whoever fights God will lose.** This is a great principle he taught me. Sometimes the whole world would be against him, but he would be standing on God's word. As we honoured him, we saw the work he had done… President Nkurunziza had a community works day. I saw him, his family and government officials get up every Saturday to go and build his country with his own people. From the day I was in Burundi, there were bullet holes because of the civil war. When I left that country 15 years later, you could hardly find them. This was the model he used to reconstruct his country: if you build it, you own it. In doing this, he taught his country to work for itself. I learnt that every individual could contribute to the building of the nation. Keep people in the strength where you need them to be not where they want to be. President and his wife had praise and worship every Sunday wherever they were. His secret service was a praise and work team as well. You must understand when you fight God, you will lose. So, God, I am sharing you my story, without God none of this is

possible in my life. I prayed to God, and he did this for me. This is my narrative. It is my truth. It is my reality. You cannot go from special needs to be an ambassador of a country that is not your own.

This photo show Sir Clyde Rivers with President Pierre Nkurunziza on a community works day in Burundi. As ambassador at large, Sir Clyde Rivers represented Burundi in various settings and occasions.

As a Global Chairman for OPAD

OPAD was founded in 2010 to reconnect the poor and marginalized communities with a global aspiration to make the world a better place for all. On this pillar, OPAD has extensively worked with donors, governments, local NGOs and the affected communities in over 40 countries to fight poverty through effective engagement on the real issues that affect the poor and marginalized people. OPAD's mission is to eradicate the problems caused by poverty, support international humanitarian laws, and promote positive climate change across all cultures. OPAD is currently working in over 40 nations. It has strong affiliations with the United Nations and the European Union.

On 30th November 2019 Sir Clyde Rivers was elected as the Global Board Chairman. Upon his election, here is the message he gave to the world:

> The world at large needs human freedom and suffering-free caused by poverty around the world. OPAD and iChange Nations believe in honoring the good individuals and nations that afford to work hard to alleviate poverty in their communities and regions. OPAD would leverage the system developed by iChange Nation with more emphasis to identify mankind that contributes in alleviating poverty, help mitigate climate change, fight against the human rights issues and protect children's right to live, by honoring them with double honor from OPAD and iChange Nations™ as well as several other institutions and organizations around the world... It is now time for individuals, institutions and other organizations to work with

OPAD to alleviation poverty, mitigate climate change, hight rights and protect the children's right to live.

HRH King Okogyeman Kobina Amissah I

As Golden Rule Ambassador

The Golden Rule International (GRI) is a relationship building organization that honours individuals and organizations for exemplifying the Golden Rule which is "Treat others the way you want to be treated." In this regard, the GRI focuses on bringing a culture of peace, harmony, constructive dialogue, and the teaching of the Golden Rule to the world irrespective of religion or none. The GRI is affiliated with the Interfaith Peace Imitative Organization (IPI). IPI is affiliated with Department of Public Information of United Nations. IPI is a member of United Religions Initiative (URI). URI is an international organization that is working throughout the world.

Recalling his appointment as a GRI Ambassador, Sir Clyde Rivers was in Kenya when he received the phone call from its then President Mussie Hailu. Recalling his appointment, he said:

> At the time, I worked with Christians only. He (Ambassador Mussie Hailu) asked me, 'I would like you to lead on the North American Division of Golden Rule International.' In my heart everything is a yes but I knew the opposition I would face. In America, are you working with Muslims? Are you working with tribal leaders? Are you working with Hindus? In my heart it was yes. This allowed me to understand spirituality. I am a great believer that the word of God is based on a kingdom not on a religion. I got the chance to watch everyone's faith and I saw that we are united by love. Ambassador Mussie Hailu told me that every major religion has a golden rule within it: treat others as you would like to be treated. If we are to have peace in the world, practice that part of your faith. With the interfaith peace building initiative, we could bring all people together under purpose of peace and not trying

> to win each other into a religion. Peace is important for where there is no peace there is no development. Peace is priceless.

Sir Clyde Rivers became a Representative to the United Nations in New York for the Interfaith Peace-Building Initiative (IPI). As a representative and activist, he Dr. Clyde Rivers works for peace. He said, "Many nations of the world do not understand the power of peace making. If you have been fortunate enough to live in a country that has never experienced war, you are a blessed person. As a peace activist for the Interfaith Peace-Building Initiative I have seen people living in total fear of what's going to happen at the end of an election. They are unsure if there will be peace or war and it causes great concern and unrest. This has become a great issue of concern for me and gives me a strong desire to initiate peace globally wherever I go." His ultimate goal is to bring peace in all communities so that people have the chance to find God.

As Godfather of World Civility

According to Sir Clyde Rivers, the Interfaith Peace Initiative opened the doors for world civility. That when he was working as the Golden Rule Ambassador, he would assemble the best people in the world that were living the golden rule and making a positive impact in their communities, and he would award them. On of his first events was at the Gerald R Ford Presidential Library in Grand Rapids, Michigan where he awarded 8 people. Six months later in the same place, he honoured 40 people from all over the world and 6 months after that honoured 120 people. Among the honorees were Dr Gordon Bradshaw and Chuck Hughes from Gary, Indiana. Later, Drs Bradshaw and Hughes launched the Community Civility Counts Initiative, created the World Civility Day, and appointed Sir Clyde Rivers as its global ambassador. This was the beginning of the world civility movement. This was the founding moment of world civility.

Sir Clyde Rivers believes that most people read about a dead great hero. However, if you did not walk with that hero in his time when he was alive, the info does not feel real to everyone. With the culture of honour that he established, it has created modern day heroes. These are the heroes that people have lived with and can see. To date, he has honoured people in over 154 countries and appointed some as civility ambassadors.

One of the world civility ambassadors is Dr Greg Dillon: Speaker, Martial Artist, and entrepreneur. He started martial arts training in 1971 and in 2019 was awarded the ultimate rank of tenth degree black belt Grandmaster Instructor in Okinawan Ryu Kyu Kempo karate by the world renowned Dillman Karate International. Dr DIllon has been authorized to carry on Professor George Dillman's legacy with his blessing. Dr Dillon has devoted much of his career to developing and implementing practical self defense and awareness programs. This led to the creation of Have a Blast with Granddad. The program is a very unique concept providing safety, civility, fitness, and nutritional information for kids of all ages. The purpose of this program is to build self esteem, confidence, and positive motivation in kids all around the world. The program follows the motto "leave your positive fingerprint on your community and have a blast!"

Dr Dillon has been named World Civility Ambassador by I Change Nations. He is a Certified Black Belt Speaker and received an Honorary Doctorate of Humanities from UGCSI. Dr Dillon is featured in 2021 Almanac of Rising Stars Newcomer of Humanity. Here is what Dr Greg Dillon, World Civility Ambassador has to say about his work with Sir Clyde Rivers.

> My work with HRH Sir Clyde Rivers has been life and career changing. His guidance and mentorship has led to so many new ideas in the areas of women and youth safety awareness. His vision in developing new ideas and concepts has been invaluable. The doors HRH has opened in the way of vision and development have progressed our project Have a Blast with Granddad and the Motorvator further and faster than ever expected. Thank you HRH for mentoring me and the friendship we have developed. We are just getting started. Have a blast!

As Godfather of World Civility, Sir Clyde Rivers has worked with entrepreneurs to establish institutions of civility around the world. One of these institutions is the Royal Civility Institute. Founded by Professor Julian Businge, The Royal Civility Institute was founded on the basis of mutual civility. By teaching and promoting civility through God's word, it pushes society closer to peace and harmony every day. It infuses the Word of God into the lives of people around the world. Its vision is to reintroduce God to people and spread his kingdom across the world through our work. It dreams of a world where everyone is a loving, compassionate, and a devoted citizen of the kingdom. Its goal is to help others uncover their true identity as children of God, and assist them with their advancement towards the kingdom of God through education, discussion, and discipline. It wants others to live holy, meaningful lives and find fulfilment in life.

Its mission states:

> The Royal Civility Institute (RCI) is an organization of scholars, leaders, and coaches that teaches the children of God different topics on divine royalty. We work tirelessly to teach others about the importance of royal civility: the consistent treatment of others with respect. We support the advancement of the Kingdom of God through theological education, the upholding of God's Holy Word, and by our actions that promote the furtherance of God's biblical worldview. Altogether, our mission is to help others understand that God is the sovereign ruler of the greatest kingdom, and show them how to follow His Word in their everyday lives.

As we end this chapter, I leave you with the words from the leaders that Sir Clyde Rivers has met in his role of taking civility around the world.

As Founder of iChange Nations

Founded by Dr. Clyde River, iChange Nations™ is a professional institution that builds diplomatic leaders by equipping, mentoring and training highly esteemed individuals who have the desire to change nations. The organization is seeking to bring global awareness by strategically helping nations to educate, train and support the nation building process designed to improve the dignity and betterment of human life. This international platform focuses on establishing effective relationships to help people understand the value of honor and basic human rights. Honour is a catalyst to recognizing greatness in others and it promotes change in communities, regions, countries and nations. This has been witnessed by Dr. Rivers and his team every time honor is bestowed upon another human being, organization, institution or government. This honor, from the office of the President of the United States, is one such experience. It is and will touch many that share in Dr. Clyde Rivers' passion to honor and spread the message of the Golden Rule.

Everywhere iChange Nations™ goes it is finding people doing good things to help mankind and people that are living the Golden Rule, "Treat others the way you want to be treated." The combined efforts of the iChange Nations™ Honor System, the Golden Rule International Award System and other organizations and institutions they work with, have catapulted iChange Nations'™ to the top. Giving them the ability to say they are the "Largest Honoring Network Establishing Cultures of Honor in the World." Soon to become the "World's Strongest Voice to Help Change the Nations."

Today, iChange Nations™ is the World's Largest Honoring Network Establishing Cultures of Honor around the world. ICN has established a system that is bringing back honor to the world. They look to honor people at global, national, state and community levels, that have made positive contributions in helping mankind. It is no wonder that Golden Rule Dialogue and honoring others are going hand-in-hand to change the world. Among the people who have received the ICN awards are presidents around the world and they include:

- President Yoweri Museveni, of Uganda – Honored for his great leadership in establishing and maintaining peace in his country;
- First Lady, Janet Museveni, of Uganda – Honored for the AIDS awareness policy ABC (Abstinence, Birth Control, and Contraception) an ever-present battle for the health of their people;
- Vice President of Kenya, Kalonzo Musyoka Honored for his efforts in the peace making process for Kenya, Sudan and Burundi;
- President Pierre Nkurunziza, of Republic of Burundi – Honored for his efforts to bring peace to a 12-year civil war between the two major tribes in his country;
- First Lady Denise Nkurunziza, Republic of Burundi Honored for her efforts to bring a better life to the people of her country;
- Former President Olusegun Obasanjo, of Nigeria – Honored for the Anticorruption policies he implemented in Nigeria;
- First Lady Maria de Luz Guebuza, of Republic of Mozambique – Honored for her humanitarian efforts for the youth and women of her country as well as bringing AIDS awareness programs;
- Former President Wolde Giorgis, of Ethiopia – Honored for his efforts to build a better environment in his country;
- Dr. Vanda Pignato – Former 1st Lady of El Salvador, was honored for her tireless efforts in protecting for women's rights in the Republic of El

Salvador;

- Dr. Kenneth David Kaunda – Former President of Zambia, was honored for his life's work to establish peace in Zambia and on the continent of Africa.

Here are some photographs of Sir Clyde Rivers with world presidents.

HRH with H.E. Wolde Giorgis, Former President of Ethiopia

Dr. Rivers with Dr Kenneth Kaunda, Former President of Zambia

Sir Clyde Rivers with President Kenneth Kaunda and Vera Chiluba, Former First Lady of Zambia

Sir Clyde Rivers with President Museveni and First Lady Janet Museveni of Uganda

Sir Clyde Rivers with Joachim Chissano, President of Mozambique

Sir Clyde Rivers with Vincente Fox Quesada,
Former President of Mexico

A DECADE OF PRESIDENTIAL HONOR
Jewel Taylor - VP Liberia / Yoweri Museveni - Pres. Uganda / Ben Shelly - former Pres Navajo Nation / Sydney Allicock - Fr VP Guyana / Vera Chiluba - First Lady Zambia / Allen Chastanet - Fr PM Saint Lucia / Pierre Nkurunziza - FR Pres Burundi / Vanda Pignato - Fr First Lady El Salvador
Jeaquim Chissano - Fr Pres Mozambique / Fatoumata Jallow-Tambajang - Fr VP Gambia / Janet Museveni - First Lady Uganda / Callista Mutharika - Fr First Lady Malawi / Mama Sarah Obama - Kenya / HRH Okogyeman Kobina Amissah I (Sir Clyde Rivers, ICN Founder)
Laurent Gbagbo - Fr Pres Ivory Coast / Maria da Luz Guebuza - Fr First Lady Mozambique / Dame Patience Jonathan - Fr First Lady Nigeria / Kalonzo Musyoka - Fr Deputy Pres Kenya / Simone Gbagbo - Fr First Lady Ivory Coast / Ranil Wickremesinghe - Sri Lanka / Ernest Bai Koroma - Fr Pres Sierra Leone
Joyce Banda - Fr Pres Malawi / Maureen Mwanawasa - Fr First Lady Zambia / Leona Marlin-Romero - Fr Prime Minister St Maarten / Olusegun Obasanjo - Fr Pres Nigeria / Denise Nkurunziza - Fr First Lady Burundi / Girma Wolde-Giorgis - Fr Pres Ethiopia

I Change Nations has not only honoured statesmen and women but also royals. Among them is the World's Youngest King Oyo Nyimba Kabamba Iguru Rukidi IV of Tooro Kingdom, Uganda.

Sultan of Sudan

Sir Rivers with Lord Eduardo Prada from Guatemala Royalty

You Walked With Me

There are a lot of people that have crossed paths with Sir Clyde Rivers on his way to the throne. As noticed in the acknowledgement section, he thanked his wife Mrs Mary Alice Rivers for her tireless support and sacrifice. Dr Robin Lococo who has been his administrator at I Change Nations for over 25 years. Chancellor Dr Michal Pitzl and Dr Donni Pitzl from the United Graduate College and Seminary International. His sister Stephanie Anne Rivers, dad and mother who taught him to dream big. Then, the international I Change Nations Family. He is forever indebted to these and all the people he has met on his long walk to the throne.

In this final chapter, we are going to focus on the contributions of President Pierre Nkurunziza and his family in Burundi, Dr Myles Monroe from the Bahamas, and Dr Albert Nasasagare from Burundi.

President Pierre Nkurunziza

Sir Clyde Rivers with H.E. Pierre Nkurunziza, President of Burundi

President Pierre Nkurunziza of Burundi is one of the people that walked with Sir Clyde Rivers. He was a principle centred leader that understood the force of living good biblical principles in place. Here is the testimony from Sir Clyde Rivers of how President Pierre Nkurunziza walked with him:

> I would be in a beautiful country and then google in the news and everything that comes out is bad. I saw for the first time in my life that you must control your media narrative. I learnt that part of the challenge of developing countries is that when you bring real knowledge, it frees people. I learnt that never build an organizations that needs poverty. Or you have to keep poverty alive to keep a job. One of the things I learnt from President Pierre is that if you want to transform a country, start with a community works day. This is the day when every Burundian would work for his/ her own country. When I first went into Burundi, there were bullets all over the walls. 15 years later, the country was transformed because of the community works day. What President Pierre Nkurunziza believed was that when you teach people how to work together, they will never tear down what they built. Every community works day, they were side by side putting bricks together. Hutus and Tutsis together with no distinction.

Dr Myles Monroe

Sir Clyde Rivers with Dr Myles Monroe, Leadership Expert

I would like to highlight the contribution of Dr Myles Monroe who impacted on Sir Clyde Rivers spiritual life. Born in 1954, Dr. Myles Munroe was a Bahamian Pastor, Teacher, Bestselling Author and International Motivational Speaker. He wrote about sixty (60) books and was a sought after Global Motivational Speaker visiting over one hundred and thirty countries. Munroe also made his greatest impact to the world as a Business Coach teaching the principles of leadership from a biblical perspective.

Dr Myles Munroe grew up in one of the poorest towns in the Bahamas where he lived with his parents and 10 siblings in a two-bedroom house. In his sermons, he narrates how in the early years, him and his brothers slept on the floor among rats and cockroaches. At the age of thirteen, he read the four Gospels and began to question if God was prejudiced. At that time the Bahamas was a British Colony and, although the population was primarily black, all the power and money were in the hands of the white minority. By fourteen years old, Munroe had memorized the four gospels that gave him a new perspective on life that nothing was impossible.

In his sermon, Dr Myles Munroe retold the story that, at age of fourteen, he found out who he was after a teacher, named Mr. Robertson from the UK called him a 'black monkey'. In fact, Munroe added that this said teacher insulted him saying that he was "retarded" and that "black people cannot learn sophisticated things." Feeling humiliated and inhumane, Myles Munroe went home and told his mother of the insults. Immediately, his mother got a Bible and instructed him to read Ephesians 3:20 which read: "Now unto him that is able to do exceedingly abundantly above all that we ask or think, according to the power that worketh in us." This new thinking changed Myles Munroe's life for the better. After realizing that the power was not in his teacher, but that it lived within him, Munroe educated himself, graduated top of the school, attended University and obtained three bachelor's degrees, a master's degree and 5 doctorates which were bestowed upon him by five different Universities.

Dr Myles Munroe recounted that one time when he had gone to England to speak at a leadership training conference. While doing book signing at the hotel where the conference took place, Myles met his former teacher Mr. Robertson who wanted him to autograph two of his books he had bought. Mr. Robertson who had by that time was very old, introduced himself to Munroe and apologized for way he treated him as a student. Munroe said that he responded to him with these words. "Mr. Robertson, don't you ever again underestimate a human." Both gentlemen hugged and kissed. This ending demonstrated the power of forgiveness and that by being success, you can silence your critics.

Dr. Munroe's ministry was based primarily on the view that everyone was born with a purpose and with gifts to be used for the betterment of humanity. "The greatest tragedy in life is not death," he wrote, "but a life without a purpose." Dr. Munroe's rise to fame was incredible and is truly an inspirational story for ordinary people to emulate or aspire to be. His life story epitomizes the saying that persons should not allow their hereditary to determine their destiny. In other words, no matter how much mankind tries to keep you down, they cannot succeed because promotion comes from God. Munroe's story gives hope to all of us who came from humble beginnings.

A regular traveller to Latin America as well as Africa, Munroe was also chief executive and chairman of the International Third World Leaders Association.

"The greatest tragedy in life is not death," he wrote, "but a life without a purpose." He believed that "Death can never kill an idea. Ideas are more powerful than death. Ideas outlive men and can never be destroyed."

He died in a plane crash along with his wife Ruth Monroe and members of his Bahama Faith Ministries on 9th November 2014. The Bahamian Prime Minister, Perry Christie, paid tribute: "It is utterly impossible to measure the magnitude of Dr Munroe's loss to the Bahamas and to the world. He was indisputably one of the most globally recognisable religious figures our nation has ever produced. His fame as an ambassador for the Christian ministry preceded him wherever in the world he travelled."

HRH Sir Clyde Rivers had the privilege of meeting Dr Myles Monroe. He was an impactful person to him as he helped him understand God's kingdom rather than religion. During the interview, he said:

> You see the kingdom of God is not a religion. Its governmental structure but people have made it a religion. The effect of it has caused major problems and that's not what Jesus was about… In the Bible, God appointed kings. A king is a governmental authority. So, Dr Myles Monroe gave me knowledge of the kingdom…

Professor Albert Nasasagare

Professor of Greatness in Diplomacy & Governance

Late one night in July 1999, Albert Nasasagare had a vision of rising and raising the youth with such strong values of servant leadership for their nation. Throughout studies at secondary school to the university, he did so by organizing seminars, workshops, crusades, mentoring, coaching and training in the area. People in the whole country and from different institutions were amazed about the versatile, visionary, and hardworking young man as a good model to his generations. The vision of that day birthed the "Youth Coalition in Action" as a non-profit organization in a bid to implement a thresh ground of the youth for a better servanthood. Today his is a Founder and Chairperson of Youth Coalition in Action (C.J.A).

Albert expanded his entrepreneurial and leadership expertise to different categories of the population, helping youth create small businesses and professional organizations have people-driven plans until October 2005 where H.E Pierre Nkurunziza, the president of the Republic of Burundi was intrigued by his spirit and endeavor and appointed him as advisor, eleven months after in September 2006, as a senior advisor and deputy Chief of State protocol. In 2012, Albert was then appointed as extraordinary and plenipotentiary ambassador of the Republic of Burundi.

Albert is a Professor of Theology at Latin University of Theology, is holding a Doctorate in Theology and two Masters Degrees International Relations and in Leadership, the three from United Graduate College and Seminary (USA), a PhD in Clinical counseling, Bachelor's Degree Financial Auditing and Management Control, and certificates in life Coaching, leadership in different African countries such as Rwanda, Ghana, Zimbabwe, Egypt, Etc.; Biblical Training Courses, in marketing and management from Bujumbura, on the subject of

Elaborating a curriculum for Youth in Secondary Schools on integrates leadership in Africa from Zimbabwe and Ghana, Etc.

Albert is a contributing Chairperson of YCA, pioneer of Community Development through a fast-result Approach, Entrepreneurial and Development coach in the youth, unemployment fighter, Etc. He has also built an Entrepreneurial Vocational Training Center in His Native Town.

In the meantime, Albert continues to make his Association a valuable and rich place for job creators in communities such as of street women, street boys, unemployed graduates; mindset transformation, micro loans provision for sustainable economies, environment protection projects, education reforms, Ethical and humanism values, leadership and civic values for the youth, health, sport, cultural disciplines and values.

At the Throne in Kuotukwa Kingdom, Ghana

King Okogyeman Obremponnsu Kobina Amissah I

HRH King Okogyeman Kobina Amissah I

The long road to the throne led to Kuotukwa Kingdom in Ghana where on 3rd of December 2021 Sir Clyde Rivers was crowned in the Republic of Ghana.

King Okogyedom Eduah V enstooled H.E. Sir Clyde Rivers to the throne of Ekumfi Kuotukwa as the Development King at Large. Sir Clyde Rivers was officially given his royal name associated with the position which is King Okogyeman Obremponnsu Kobina Amissah I.

He was introduced to the world on the 3rd of December 2021 in front of a packed house. Delegates from several countries, kings, queens, and other royalty witnessed his enstoolment. After his coronation, HRH gave a speech that outlined his vision of developing Kuotukwa Kingdom.

HRH King Okogyeman Kobina Amissah I

A Long Walk to the Throne

There is no better way to end this book than using the very words of Sir Clyde Rivers:

> Dr Patrick Businge, it has been a long walk to the throne. From my ancestors that came at the bottom of a slave boat in the sea to me; from me being labelled special education to coming to Africa in a first-class flight as a King of Development. Now, to have walked through from being a pastor through honorary ambassador to being promoted as a king. I never imagined being ambassador to a country that is not my own. I never imagined being a king in a kingdom that was not my own. Dr Businge, I know no other story like this. It is all because of God. I have asked Jesus and he led me in my life from where I was to where I am now. It is a miracle. This was my long walk to the throne that I am called to occupy and make the lives of others better.

I had my wife Mary Alice Rivers has stood everything I do. As this book finishes, she will have her doctorate in education from Grand Canyon University in Arizona. I had people that had stayed with me. My sister Stephanie Rivers. Every leader will have moments when they are crying for someone to pick you up. I was humbled when I received the actual call to be the development king at large in Ghana.

A Legacy of Greatness

GREATNESS UNIVERSITY

LONDON, UK

As we come to the end of this book, you might have noticed that Sir Clyde Rivers has followed a long journey to the throne. Keeping in mind of his ancestry as a grandson of the African soil, his journey to the throne has made him to pass through various roles such as Dean of UGCSI, Ambassador at Large for Burundi, Golden Rule Ambassador, and Godfather of World Civility. This is truly a reflection of a true legend of greatness. Along his path, Sir Clyde Rivers has touched the hearts and souls of people. He has inspired people for eternity because she sought the kingdom of God first. He has created history that is going to remain relevant until the God comes with his kingdom. Sir Clyde Rivers has reminded us that we are there to change humanity through service. Indeed, he has made people better every single day.

This is a clear testament that legacy is not about making yourself great but make others great. Legacy is the pinnacle of greatness. The philosopher William James said that "The great use of life is to spend it for something that will outlast it." For most people what will outlast them is not property, possessions or money. For them, legacy is not leaving something for people. According to the most connected man in America Peter Strople, legacy is leaving something in people. The legacy you leave is the life you live. You leave a legacy by leading out of your life and not out of your position. So, legends of greatness like Sir Clyde Rivers work towards replicating their greatness in the people they inspire and come into contact with. They focus on multiplying their successors. In most cases, the successors of Legends of Greatness become more successful than them. What happens in their absence becomes the measure of their greatness. Organisations that Legends of Greatness leave behind become more successful after they have gone. Legacy creators are obsessed with replication.

Many people think that legacy is only for the rich and famous. Legacy is a reflection of how you live your life. It is composed of the dreams, values, vision, creations, etc that you pass on to the future generations. Based on this understanding everyone has the potential to leave a good or bad legacy. Legends of Greatness replicate good legacy. For example, today we associate The Nobel Prize with Alfred Nobel. Born into poverty, Alfred Nobel become one of the prominent chemists and inventors of the 19th century. Alfred invented dynamite, various explosives, and amassed over 355 patents. During his time, the press referred to him as the 'merchant' and 'angel of death'. His turning point came in 1888 when his brother Ludvig died. A French journalist believed that it was Alfred who had died and wrote the headline: 'Le marchand de la mort est mort' which means 'The merchant of death is dfead.' Alfred Nobel was deeply affected by this premature obituary, and it led him to reflect on his legacy.

Having read this obituary which condemned him for profiting from the sales of arms, scared of leaving a bad legacy as the angel of death, Alfred Nobel wrote in his last will in Paris on 27th November 1895 that the bulk of his $300 million fortune should be used for prizes in physics, chemistry, physiology or medicine, literature and peace to "those who, during the preceding year, shall have conferred the greatest benefit to humankind." This was the birth of Nobel Prizes.

So, imagine that your life is ended abruptly right now and tomorrow would be a world without you. What obituary would be published about you in your national newspaper? If it is not as you would like it to be, what do you need to do to leave a great and replicable legacy? Is it writing the book, starting a business, volunteering, praying more, donating your wealth to charity, reconciling with your enemies, loving more, being more present to your family, writing your memoir so that your family would have a story about your life? You might wish to take action today to create your legacy and sustain your greatness.

There is a common saying that the power of a person's life is the stories they leave behind. In order to replicate legacy, you need a great story about you. This could be a story of struggle, love, loss, success in the midst of the challenges of life, etc. The building blocks of your story could include your selfless service, virtues, values, spirituality, talents, gifts, and as we shall see, your legacy is your ubuntu. Your values allow you to live for a cause greater than yourself. Your spirituality allows you to attain downward greatness. Your challenges allow you to be more caring and compassionate. You need faith to be able to replicate a lasting legacy. It is because of his persistence in the journey that he as walked to his throne, we at Greatness University have created an award in his honour.

Greatness University is the world's first and only institution dedicated to researching greatness in individuals, institutions and systems. It also offers a breakthrough education that helps people discover, develop and deliver their greatness. This breakthrough education which synchronies real-time greatness, impactful authorship, and traditional academia is delivered through our virtual institutes and affiliate partners globally.

In addition to research and education, we create new authors. At Greatness University, we will help you publish your work with Greatness University Publications. This publishing arm includes *Greatness University Publishers* for books, *Greatness University Journals* for articles, and the *World Book of Greatness* for profiles and biographies of great people. Through Greatness University Publications, we provide the global exposure and influence you deserve. For a list of our publications and to see how you can publish with us, visit www.greatnessuniversity.co.uk

We recognise that the world is filled with unsung heroes and heroines. More often, their greatness is never celebrated when they are alive. In this respect, we have created the *World Greatness Day*: an occasion to recognise, honour and celebrate people who have helped us to positively change our lives whilst they are alive. Get in touch if you need more information. We look forward to helping you make your greatness tangible.

Distinguished Honours to Sir Clyde Rivers: Presidential Greatness Award

Bibliography

Burum F.B, (2020). *The Sorrows of Slavery: Poetry of the Past.* London: Greatness University Publishers.

Businge, P, (2020). *Greatness Code.* London: Greatness University Publishers.

Mbiti, J.S. (1970). *African Religions and Philosophy.* London: Heinemann.

Otto, R. (1917). *The Idea of the Holy.*

Wilkinson, G.S., & Robertson, G.J. (2006). *WRAT4 wide range achievement test: Professional Manual.* Florida: PAR.

Africa before Transatlantic Enslavement - Black History Month 2021

https://www.einpresswire.com/article/558460130/h-e-sir-clyde-rivers-coronation-day

Photo Credits

- Cover Photo: Royal Civility Institute
- Clyde Rivers Facebook Page
- Benjamin Franklin Burum
- Ernest Bai Koroma Twitter
- Greatness University

CPSIA information can be obtained
at www.ICGtesting.com
Printed in the USA
LVHW072145220422
716976LV00010B/223

* 9 7 8 1 9 1 3 1 6 4 1 5 7 *